HAMILTON

FRANK KEATING

PAINTINGS BY

MIKE WIMMER

A Paula Wiseman Book

SIMON & SCHUSTER BOOKS FOR YOUNG READERS
NEW YORK LONDON TORONTO SYDNEY NEW DELHI

All quotes used in this book are accurate and attributed to Alexander Hamilton.

The illustrator gratefully acknowledges everyone at Colonial Williamsburg who keeps history alive and who helped with the research for this book. And in addition, grateful acknowledgment to Catherine Whittenburg for her generosity and patience in helping to bring authenticity and historical accuracy to these pages.

SIMON & SCHUSTER BOOKS FOR YOUNG READERS
An imprint of Simon & Schuster Children's Publishing Division
1230 Avenue of the Americas, New York, New York 10020

The text for this book was set in Adobe Caslon Pro.
The illustrations for this book were rendered in oil on canvas.
Manufactured in Guangdong province, China
0421 SCP
First Simon & Schuster Books for Young Readers POB proprietary edition April 2021
10 9 8 7 6 5 4 3 2 1
Library of Congress Cataloging-in-Publication Data
Names: Keating, Francis Anthony, 1944– author. | Wimmer, Mike, illustrator.
Title: Hamilton / Frank Keating ; illustrated by Mike Wimmer.
Description: New York : Simon & Schuster Books for Young Readers, [2020] |
Audience: Ages 4–8 | Audience: Grades 2–3 | Summary: "A picture book biography of
Alexander Hamilton's life from boyhood to becoming a Founding Father."— Provided by publisher.
Identifiers: LCCN 2019052790 (print) | LCCN 2019052791 (eBook) |
ISBN 9781534406568 (hardcover) | ISBN 9781534406575 (eBook)
Subjects: LCSH: Hamilton, Alexander, 1757–1804—Juvenile literature. | Statesmen—United States—Biography—Juvenile literature. | United States—Politics and government—1783–1809—Juvenile literature.
Classification: LCC E302.6.H2 K43 2020 (print) | LCC E302.6.H2 (eBook) |
DDC 973.4092 [B]—dc23
LC record available at https://lccn.loc.gov/2019052790
LC eBook record available at https://lccn.loc.gov/2019052791

America's extraordinary story was first told by its founders. To proclaim independence and to face and defeat the greatest military power of the age was extraordinary. All from an idea. Our founders sacrificed everything for liberty. This book is dedicated to those long-dead, courageous souls.

—F. K.

I want to dedicate this book to all those born out of privilege who create their own opportunities through hard work, dedication to education, and the ability to reinvent themselves after failure.

—M. W.

I was a Father of my country. I was there when we became a free and sovereign nation. Not more than a boy, I wrote pamphlets supporting the cause of liberty. I spoke in the streets. Though we were a colony, I said that all men have a right to govern themselves.

"The sacred rights of mankind . . . are written, as with a sunbeam . . . by the hand of the divinity itself."

I argued. I wrote. I was at the center, the passion and fire, of the creation of a new land.

But my life was not expected to be that way.

I was born on January 11, 1755. Not in America, but in a small town on the island of Nevis in the West Indies. In the Caribbean, where I gloried in the smell of cinnamon, nutmeg, avocado, and ginger root. Around me was the sea, and on the land were whirring windmills that crushed sugarcane, the principal crop of my island home. My friends and I hiked through fields and scenes sprinkled with smells of yams, sweet potatoes, smoked ham, and fresh fish. Everywhere were the colorful and wild aloe vera plants, a common sight in the tropics.

As a child, I attended a small Hebrew school, though I was largely homeschooled. My mother taught me French. She also taught me the Ten Commandments. I was small and frequently was placed on a table to stand and recite.

When I was ten years old, we moved to Saint Croix, another island in the Caribbean.

My mother became a shopkeeper and I became a part-time clerk. We kept a goat for milk. I minded the store and kept the books and watched the inventory.

And then my happiness ended. My mother died. My brother and I were orphaned and penniless.

I lived as I could. At age twelve, I was on my own. I began to read, and read all that I could from the small library that my mother left me. Alexander Pope. Plutarch. I learned math and chemistry. I learned about money and marketing. I began to write poetry. I also learned that I would rise in the world only through education and hard work. I read. And learned. And worked. I was noticed by leading businessmen on Saint Croix, who raised the money to permit me to complete my education. I sailed to America, never to return to the Caribbean.

I was seventeen.

I settled in New York City and became a college student.

I studied the Bible. I also studied geography, literature, speech, Greek, and Latin. I also plunged into the debates that roiled the land. We may be British colonies but we have the rights of Englishmen. Shall we be free or shall a faraway land tell us what to do? I argued that no law was just without the will of the people. I wrote essays. I raced through my studies and pursued the cause of liberty. I was all action.

"I cannot make everyone as rapid as myself." Few worked as hard as I. I was a whirlwind.

The revolution began. Clash and combat. A war between colony and mother country. For the rights of all people. For independence. I was still young, without family or fortune. "I am a stranger in the country. I have no property here, no connections."

I was a private in a New York militia company.

I was the captain of an artillery company.

I was a lieutenant colonel on the staff of General George Washington.

I was the "Little Lion." "Ham" or "Hammie" to my friends. I fought the enemy and was indifferent to danger. I became a war hero.

The war ended. The revolution was won. It was now time to build a nation.

But how to do it? We were young and poor, divided by thirteen different state governments and thirteen different systems of law. I became a lawyer and soon was a member of the New York Assembly and a member of the congress of the states. I argued for a strong national government with the power to tax. The government had little money to pay its bills. The country needed a standing army, a navy, a coast guard.

The strength to protect its people. And money that was more than worthless paper.

"Power without revenue . . . is a bubble."

I quickly set to work. Vigor and action from me. Vigor and action for a new government. In 1789, I was still in my early thirties. I was the leading voice to call for a convention of the states to give a national congress and a national government all powers that relate to war, peace, trade, and a national currency. I argued for the creation of a national bank that would take deposits and loan money to the government to fund warships, roads, bridges, and canals. All the national needs of a strong and proud people.

"There is no time for a wrong decision. These days must be the last stage of national humiliation."

Beginning in 1787, I wrote most of the Federalist Papers, which made the argument for a strong government with three strong branches, including a strong president and an independent court system.

The states agreed, and today's government was formed.

"It's not tyranny we desire; it's a just, limited federal government."

Some of my joyous New York neighbors even called for my city to be renamed "Hamiltoniana."

The man whom I admired above all others, George Washington, became the first president of the United States. He asked me to be the first secretary of the treasury. I had the vision and the energy to right the government's finances. I set the dollar as the national currency. I formed the Customs Service. I encouraged the creation of banks so that commerce would flourish.

"Men give me credit for some genius. All the genius I have lies in this: when I have a subject in hand, I study it profoundly. Day and night it is before me.

It is the fruit of labor and thought."

I called for prizes for inventions and new life for manufacturers and agriculture. I urged the creation of a city for manufacturers, which became Paterson, New Jersey.

I demanded high ethical standards in government and set the stage for the modern civil service. I was the Father of the American government.

"The honor of a nation is its life."

When I took office, the United States was bankrupt. When I left office six years later, we were prosperous, with sound public credit, a stable government, and a working Constitution.

When my life in government and at George Washington's side ended, I was a poor man. My joy and wife, Eliza, and our eight children sacrificed for me. I sacrificed for my country.

"I am not worth exceeding $500 in the world. My slender fortune and the best years of my life have been devoted to the service of my adopted country."

I continued to fight for all people of every color and was a strong believer in merit as the foundation of success.

"I think the first duty of society is justice."

I championed the creation of a professional army and served as inspector general and a major general.

I assisted in founding the oldest surviving newspaper in America, the New York *Evening Post*.

I helped form two banks. I founded the Coast Guard.

I also made time for the outdoors, hunting with my special retriever, Old Peggy.

I enjoyed the theater, symphony, and walking the streets of my favorite young city, New York.

Mine was a life of enormous consequence that, by accident, I, an immigrant, could find in America a land that loved me as much as I loved her.

Author's Note

Alexander Hamilton was an unknown immigrant, an orphan, a boy of no connections and little promise who helped transform the world. At Washington's side, he helped bring victory to the American cause, wrote most of the Federalist Papers, and helped to create the prosperous colossus that is the United States. Sadly, on July 11, 1804, Hamilton was shot in a duel with Aaron Burr, the sitting vice president, on the New Jersey side of the Hudson River. Hamilton was carried back to New York City where he died. His legacy survives to this day.

Bibliography

Chernow, Ron. *Alexander Hamilton*. New York: Penguin Press, 2004.

Ellis, Joseph J. *The Quartet: Orchestrating the Second American Revolution, 1783–1789*. New York: Vintage, 2015.

Flexner, James Thomas. *Washington: The Indispensable Man*. New York: Back Bay Books, 1994.

Hamilton, Alexander, John Jay, and James Madison. *The Federalist Papers*. CreateSpace Independent Publishing Platform, 2019.

Randall, Willard Sterne. *Alexander Hamilton: A Life*. New York: Harper Collins, 2003.

Sylla, Richard. *Alexander Hamilton: The Illustrated Biography*. New York: Sterling Books, 2018.

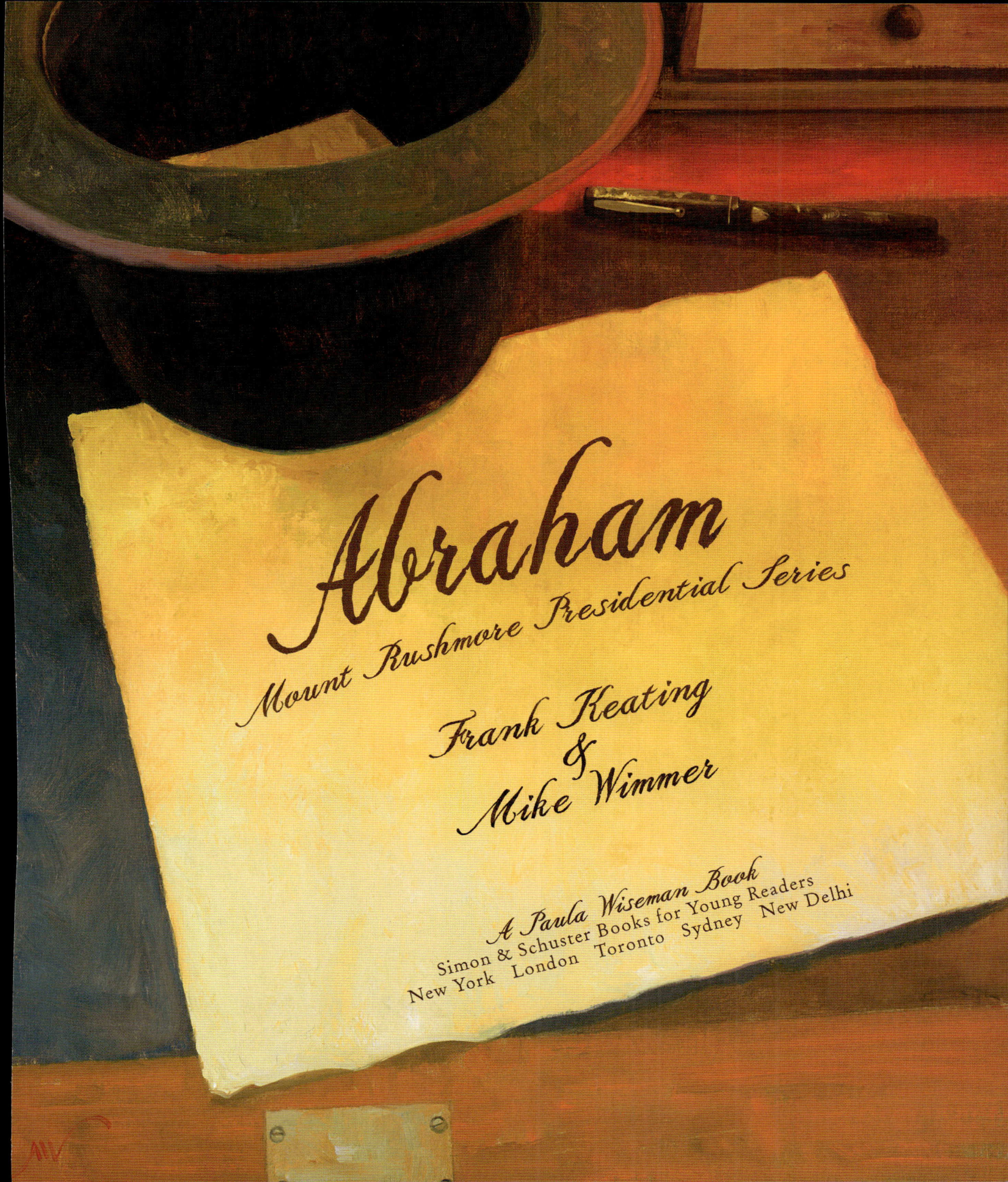
Abraham
Mount Rushmore Presidential Series
Frank Keating
&
Mike Wimmer
A Paula Wiseman Book
Simon & Schuster Books for Young Readers
New York London Toronto Sydney New Delhi

FOR WHOM HE SAVED THE UNION
THE MEMORY OF ABRAHAM LINCOLN
IS ENSHRINED FOREVER

Father Abraham.

Honest Abe.

The Great Emancipator.

I was also the sixteenth president of the United States of America.

I liberated the slaves.

I saved the Union.

Early on, though, I wasn't expected to amount to much.

"It is a great piece of folly to attempt to make anything out of my early life."

It really can be summarized by a single phrase. My childhood was a part of the "short and simple annals of the poor."

There was little that could be said about me because "there [was] not much of me."

I was born on February 12, 1809, in a Kentucky cabin with a packed-dirt floor, rough slab roof, and a leather-hinged door, all held in place by poles and stones.

It had one room and a single window.

My clothes were sewn from cloth spun by my mother or fashioned from the skin of animals shot by my father. I helped with the chores. I carried water from the creek. I hoed weeds, picked berries, and grubbed for walnuts, hickory, and hazelnuts.

Our suppers were simple and mostly wild game: turkey, partridge, rabbit, deer, and bear.

I walked barefoot for most of the year, through all the seasons.

I saw myself as "humble Abraham Lincoln" because "I was born and have ever remained in the most humble walks of life."

I went to school "by littles." All together, it did not amount to one year. Our books were few but important: the Bible, Webster's *Spelling Book*, and *Pike's Arithmetic.*

Books opened my eyes. They captured my mind.

Reading was everything to me.

As I grew tall and strong, I worked hard. I cleared timber for pastures for livestock and corn. I burned brush, split rails, milked cows, churned butter, and cured hides of raccoon and deer.

Heavy toil.

Hard work is the most persistent memory of my youth.

My free time was consumed by books. Any books. All books. Through thicket and thorn I scoured for books. I once walked twenty miles to borrow a book.

"The things I want to know are in books."

I also read and wrote poetry and rhyme. My pen was a turkey buzzard feather tipped with ink from a blackberry briar root. Sometimes I wrote silly verses: "Abraham Lincoln, his hand and pen, he will be good but God knows when."

From Kentucky to Indiana and eventually to Illinois. As my family moved, my circle remained those that I loved. And my books. I read and memorized what I could. If I had no paper to write on, I used wooden boards.

I loved to be with people. I occasionally jumped onto a tree stump or stood on a fence to talk to my fellow workers. My father frequently made me stop to return to work.

I often traveled across the Ohio River and down the Mississippi–running a ferryboat or a flatboat for goods. I continued to learn. I listened to speeches; I heard legal arguments in court. I was alert to new ideas. I absorbed it all: by sight, by scent, by sound.

In Illinois, I worked as a store clerk. I read late and arose early to read. I always carried a book under my arm. When I was the postmaster of New Salem, I carried the mail in my hat. I also worked as a surveyor, a storekeeper, a mill hand, a soldier, and a legislator.

I continued to read. And to study. And to debate the issues of the day. I became a lawyer without legal training, which was often remarked upon as the envy of many.

I moved to Springfield and studied the law, seated at a rough wooden table, warmed by an old woodstove and a buffalo hide.

The law was my love. I resolved to be a peacemaker. I vowed to make good morals a part of my law practice. I determined "to be honest at all events." I believed that if one cannot be an honest lawyer, he should at least "resolve to be honest without being a lawyer."

I knew that hard work was my only path. Truthfulness and fair dealing in law and in business resulted in my being called Honest Abe.

I prospered as a lawyer and met Mary, married, and became a father. My neighbors continued to trust and respect me. They elected me to a brief term in Congress.

My ambition was simple and straightforward: to be "truly esteemed of my fellow man."

But the times were unsettled. Passion and controversy roiled the land.

Everywhere, people began to ask whether it was right that one man could own another. Some said that ownership of one by another was protected by the Constitution. Others argued that the Union promised a new life for ordinary people, free and limited only by the imagination and ambition of its citizens.

I believed that the Declaration of Independence was a "charter of freedom" for all people.

"He who would be no slave, must consent to have no slave. Those who deny freedom to others, deserve it not for themselves. . . ."

"If slavery is not wrong, nothing is wrong."

I was determined to secure freedom for others and to assure the union of our states.

Freedom and union had pulled me up from a "hired" laborer, little better than a slave, to a "society of equals." I could not stand by and see it end.

I knew that "there can be no moral right with one man making a slave of another."

Though not in office, I would not remain silent. The country was ablaze with emotion and conflict. It appeared that disunion and slavery would shatter our splintering land.

I stood for one people and one land. I traveled the country. I entered the fray. My voice was heard. People listened. I was elected the sixteenth president of the United States. People were convinced a "house divided" cannot stand. Our wonderful land could not remain half slave and half free.

Though I hoped the "better angels of our nature" would hold us together, I was wrong. The country broke apart.

Blue versus gray. North versus South. Brother versus brother. War and bloodshed. The agony appeared endless.

Defeat. Darkness. Destruction. And from some, despair.

"We cannot escape history. . . . The fiery trial through which we pass, will light us down, in honor or dishonor, to the latest generation."

But I always knew that this nation, under God, would survive. We were "the last, best hope of earth." America must survive. America must prevail.

My goal never changed. My resolve never faltered.

Union and freedom. Forever.

"With malice toward none, with charity for all," the nation would become one again.

A
12

The sparkling call for equality and dignity for each person emblazoned in the Declaration of Independence would be embraced by all and enjoyed by all, now and tomorrow.

This conflict was a "people's contest," to "elevate the condition of men . . ."—all men—"to afford all an unfettered start and a fair chance, in the race of life."

The Civil War was finally won. The experiment was nobly saved.

The Union survived.

Every man was free.

Man's best hopes of equal opportunity and equal rights would not perish from the earth.

Address Delivered at the Dedication of the Cemetery at Gettysburg

Abraham Lincoln

NOVEMBER 19, 1863

Four score and seven years ago our fathers brought forth on this continent, a new nation, conceived in Liberty, and dedicated to the proposition that all men are created equal.

Now we are engaged in a great civil war, testing whether that nation, or any nation so conceived and dedicated, can long endure. We are met on a great battlefield of that war. We have come to dedicate a portion of that field, as a final resting place for those who here gave their lives that that nation might live. It is altogether fitting and proper that we should do this.

But, in a larger sense, we cannot dedicate—we cannot consecrate—we cannot hallow—this ground. The brave men, living and dead, who struggled here, have consecrated it, far above our poor power to add or detract. The world will little note, nor long remember what we say here, but it can never forget what they did here. It is for us the living, rather, to be dedicated here to the unfinished work which they who fought here have thus far so nobly advanced. It is rather for us to be here dedicated to the great task remaining before us—that from these honored dead we take increased devotion to that cause for which they gave the last full measure of devotion—that we here highly resolve that these dead shall not have died in vain—that this nation, under God, shall have a new birth of freedom—and that government of the people, by the people, for the people, shall not perish from the earth.

The life of Abraham Lincoln was an affirmation of the unprecedented call of the Declaration of Independence that all men are created equal. Unheard of when written and marked by reverses and resistance since its utterance, it remains the fundamental law of the land. This book is dedicated to those who have stood for equality since Lincoln's day. To those who have lived with firmness and resolve that race, color, sex, and nationality can play no role in halting the progress of all to be one.

—F. K.

To my three sons, Eli, Holden, and Broden, who have all helped to bring Abraham alive by modeling for me. I hope that he will also be a model for you.

—M. W.

ACKNOWLEDGMENTS

The illustrator gratefully acknowledges Dan Storck, supervisor of Mount Vernon, who modeled as President Lincoln, and Hilary Malson, marketing and membership coordinator for President Lincoln's Cottage, a Site of the National Trust for Historic Preservation, for their help in researching and creating this book.

BIBLIOGRAPHY

There are many great books on Abraham Lincoln. This is a list of those I referred to while writing this book.—F. K.

Beveridge, Albert J. *Abraham Lincoln 1809–1858.* Vol. 1. Boston: Houghton Mifflin, 1928.

Gallagher, Gary W. *The Union War*. Cambridge, MA: Harvard University Press, 2011.

Guelzo, Allen C. "Our Lincoln." *National Review*. February 23, 2009.

Lincoln, Abraham. *Lincoln: Speeches and Writings 1832–1858.* Edited by Don E. Fehrenbacher. New York: Library of America, 1989.

McPherson, James M. *Abraham Lincoln and the Second American Revolution*. London: Oxford University Press, 1991.

Nicolay, John G. *A Short Life of Abraham Lincoln*. New York: The Century Company, 1903.

Pratt, Harry E. *Concerning Mr. Lincoln*. Springfield, IL: Abraham Lincoln Association, 1944.

Sandburg, Carl. *Abraham Lincoln: The Prairie Years.* New York: Harcourt Brace, 1926.

Simon, Paul. *Lincoln's Preparation for Greatness*. Norman, OK: OU Press, 1965.

Thomas, Benjamin P. *Abraham Lincoln: A Biography.* New York: Modern Library, 1968.

Wilson, Douglas L. *Honor's Voice: The Transformation of Abraham Lincoln*. New York: Knopf, 1999.

All quotations are the words of Abraham Lincoln.

SIMON & SCHUSTER BOOKS FOR YOUNG READERS
An imprint of Simon & Schuster Children's Publishing Division • 1230 Avenue of the Americas, New York, New York 10020

Book design by Chloë Foglia © 2017 by Simon & Schuster, Inc. • The text for this book was set in Old Claude. • The illustrations for this book were rendered in oil on canvas.
Manufactured in Guangdong province, China • 0421 SCP • First Simon & Schuster Books for Young Readers POB proprietary edition April 2021
2 4 6 8 10 9 7 5 3 1
Library of Congress Cataloging-in-Publication Data
Names: Keating, Francis Anthony, 1944– | Wimmer, Mike, illustrator.
Title: Abraham / Frank Keating ; illustrated by Mike Wimmer.
Description: 1st edition. | New York : Simon & Schuster Books for Young Readers, 2017. | Series: A Paula Wiseman book
Identifiers: LCCN 2013015823| ISBN 9781442493193 (hardcover) | ISBN 9781442493209 (eBook)
Subjects: LCSH: Lincoln, Abraham, 1809–1865—Juvenile literature. | Presidents—United States—Biography—Juvenile literature.
Classification: LCC E457.905 .K43 2017 | DDC 973.7092—dc23 LC record available at http://lccn.loc.gov/2013015823

GEORGE

George Washington, Our Founding Father

FRANK
KEATING

Paintings by
MIKE
WIMMER

A Paula Wiseman Book
Simon & Schuster Books for Young Readers
NEW YORK LONDON TORONTO SYDNEY NEW DELHI

The author, illustrator, and publisher gratefully acknowledge the Mount Vernon Ladies' Association for their help in creating this book.

SIMON & SCHUSTER BOOKS FOR YOUNG READERS • An imprint of Simon & Schuster Children's Publishing Division 1230 Avenue of the Americas, New York, New York 10020 • Text © 2012 by Frank Keating • Illustrations

• For information about special discounts for bulk purchases, please contact Simon & Schuster Special Sales at 1-866-506-1949 or business@simonandschuster.com. • The Simon & Schuster Speakers Bureau can bring authors to your live event. • For more information or to book an event, contact the Simon & Schuster Speakers Bureau at 1-866-248-3049 or visit our website at www.simonspeakers.com. • Book design by Chloë Foglia © 2012 by Simon & Schuster, Inc. The text for this book is set in Celestia Antiqua Std. • The illustrations for this book are rendered in oil on canvas. • Manufactured in Guangdong province, China • 0421SCP • First Simon & Schuster Books for Young Readers POB proprietary edition April 2021

2 4 6 8 10 9 7 5 3 1

Library of Congress Cataloging-in-Publication Data • Keating, Francis Anthony, 1944– • George : George Washington, our founding father / Frank Keating ; illustrated by Mike Wimmer. • p. cm. • Summary: "The fifth of ten children, George Washington was a dreamer, a hard worker, an athlete, and a peacemaker. By the time he was fifteen he had handwritten for himself the "Rules of Civility and Decent Behavior in Company and Conversation." These were his rules to live by. He could not have known what his future would hold . . . and these rules speak to who he was as a boy and a man. Based on this little known historical document, this is George Washington's life from boyhood to his presidency"—Provided by publisher. Includes bibliographical references. • ISBN 978-1-4169-5482-8 (hardcover) • 1. Washington, George, 1732-1799—Juvenile literature. 2. Presidents—United States—Biography—Juvenile literature. I. Wimmer, Mike, ill. II. Title. III. Title: George Washington, our founding father. • E312.66.K43 2012 • 973.4'1092—dc23 • [B] • 2011013322 • ISBN 978-1-4424-4717-2 (eBook)

Editor's Note: All quotations are the words of George Washington. Archaic spelling, capitalization, and punctuation in historical quotations have been modernized throughout the text.

My special grandchildren, Catie, Will, Matthew, Hadley, Emma, Chloe, Callie, Mary Frances, and Frank, are young Americans who will soon learn of the luster and legacy of our nation's first president. This book is dedicated to them. But it is also dedicated to the regents, vice regents, and staff of Mount Vernon, without whose professionalism and devotion to Washington's memory, the light of the nation's father would be considerably dimmed.

—F.K.

For Paula Wiseman, whose guidance and friendship have given me a voice with which I can speak to the ages

—M.W.

I am remembered as the Father of My Country.
The indispensable man.

First in War.

First in Peace.

First in the hearts of my countrymen.

Rule 110:

Labor to keep alive in your breast that little spark of celestial fire called conscience.

First I was a child.

I was born February 22, 1732, the fifth of ten children. My Virginia birthplace was a house built on a bed of oyster shells. My parents were Augustine and Mary Ball Washington. To my great sadness, my father died when I was eleven.

In school I studied hard. Arithmetic. Penmanship. Reading. I began to write a list of rules that my teachers taught me. Rules of character that I knew I must always remember.

At play I was tall and strong. Frequently I was asked to be the peacemaker. I formed a company of boy soldiers at school. I was chosen captain and spent hours of fun marching my friends across the grass.

Rule 73:

Think before you speak. Pronounce not imperfectly nor bring out your words too hastily, but orderly and distinctly.

When my classmates and I had no books to read, we entertained ourselves by memorizing the names and verses from old tombstones.

Some were quite funny:

"John Hizer,
The Mizer,
Is wiser—we hope."

Rule 74:

When another speaks, be attentive yourself and disturb not the audience. If any hesitate in his words, help him not nor prompt him without desired, interrupt him not, nor answer him till his speech be ended.

At age fifteen my formal education ended. Though "defective" to my mind, it was not unusual for children of my time to finish school at a young age. Since my father had passed away, I was expected to help my mother care for our large family.

Rule 56:

Associate yourself with men of good quality if you esteem your own reputation, for 'tis better to be alone than in bad company.

When I left school, I became a surveyor. I was also a blacksmith and a carpenter. I could make a barrel about as well as a cooper could. My work became a classroom of life lessons. I learned from experience.

I grew by reading and observing. Good manners bred good morals. And good morals produced a respected and successful adult. I applied the "Rules of Civility" to all that I did. I put them to practice. They were my primer on life. I first learned them in school. I wrote them down. They became a part of me.

Rule 82:

Undertake not what you cannot perform but be careful to keep your promise.

In my twenties I was in the midst of the action. I was a major of militia. I was "bent to arms," and volunteered to lead a party through nine hundred miles of wilderness to deliver a message to the French. I was young, but I was trusted.

Rule 35:

Let your discourse with men of business be short and comprehensive.

I was trained and confident. I was selected to lead. The weather was bone-chilling. I parleyed with Indians. A bullet fired "not fifteen steps" away nearly struck me. I was thrown into a swift roaring river and almost drowned. But my strength and will to survive saved me. For months I withstood cold and hardship, yet I accomplished my mission and came home a respected and wiser man.

Rule 1:

Every action done in company ought to be with some sign of respect to those that are present.

Later I returned to the woods and accompanied our English forces on a mission to eject the French from their claims to the Ohio Valley. The battle was the opening of a worldwide seven-year war that would drive the French from North America and place our British cousins firmly in charge of the continent. "I heard the bullets whistle," I wrote. Four bullet holes were in my coat and two horses were wounded under me. A lead ball passed through my hat. Our effort was unsuccessful, but I had done my boldest and best. I came home a hero.

At age twenty-seven I married Martha, a widow and mother of two children, Patsy and Jacky. I had no children of my own.

My principles were clear. The lesson plan was straightforward. "The Rules of Civility" had been a part of me since I copied them when I was fifteen. They sustained me through the birth of our nation.

When Virginia and the other colonies began the great debate for independence, I was there.

I wore my uniform to the sessions of Congress. I was unanimously selected as commander in chief of our armies. I devoted myself solely to "American union and patriotism."

Rule 44:

When a man does all he can, though it succeeds not well, blame not him that did it.

I remembered the advice of my youth.

I kept my promise. I was the first soldier commissioned by my country. I remained in the army and did not return home until each battle was won.

Darkness and defeat. Success and uncertainty. But never despair. The virtue of my men and the nobility of our cause would ultimately bring our reward.

God was an active agent in all that we were attempting.

Rule 108:

When you speak of God or His attributes, let it be seriously and with reverence.

Our prayers were answered. This "wonderful Revolution" was won, and those who would treat us as slaves were forced from our shores.

But the ending was just the beginning. The new nation was weak.

We had national "character" to establish. The country needed to defend liberty and provide for representative government. "The preservation of the sacred fire of liberty and the destiny of the republican model of government" were staked on this experiment. A constitutional convention was called. I was unanimously chosen as its president. We began our task.

Finally our work was done. The Constitution, few in words, created a national government while limiting the powers of that government. It was a document devoted to the common good.

When the states accepted the Constitution, I was unanimously elected as our country's first president, and then elected again for a second term.

I led a great people. To make a great land.

To create a better world.

Author's Note

George Washington, our founding father, led us to independence in the Revolutionary War and was the first president of our nation. He was born in 1732, and though no photographs of him exist, one way we can understand him is through the "Rules of Civility" he copied as a young schoolboy with the help of his teachers in Virginia. These are rules that George Washington compiled to guide his life. For a complete list of the rules, visit gwpapers.virginia.edu.

As a young boy, George Washington couldn't have known he would become the first president of a new country, but the seeds of leadership and greatness were planted in his early years. It is my hope that by my sharing some of the incidents of young George Washington's life, made all the more real by Mike Wimmer's glowing paintings, you will have a better understanding of who George Washington was and how his life was shaped to influence our country and our lives so many years later.

Artist's Note

The paintings for this book were created using oil paints on canvas. I first generated a number of sketches to create interesting compositions to bring the viewer into the story, as if we were a direct witness to the events that molded the character of America's first president, George Washington. I did this by employing models to portray the characters. I then chose the correct lighting that would best amplify the quiet drama of each moment. Then I created completely finished sketches before I transferred the image to canvas. My under painting was usually done in a monochromatic value that best reflected the mood of the scene. I then finished the painting, concentrating on the focal point of the narrative, utilizing contrast of color, value, or brushwork.

Each painting was meticulously researched for costume accuracy and setting. Paintings of the period were an enormous help. I engrossed myself with the details of George's life, and he became more real to me. This allowed me to better portray him as a human being rather than the iconic figure he has become through myth and legend.

I want to thank a few of the people and organizations that helped me bring this project to fruition. James C. Rees, executive director of Mount Vernon, and the regents and staff allowed me unfettered access to the grounds and artifacts that enabled me to reproduce with such accuracy. Thanks also to the dedicated group of re-enactors at the Fort Loudoun State Historic Area in Vonore, Tennessee. Whit Edwards and other re-enactors of the Oklahoma History Center were invaluable in bringing to life the period of the revolution.

It was indeed a challenge and an honor to bring to life this heroic character. I want each of the readers to come away with a deep respect for this common man, who made uncommon choices that positioned our small country for the greatness that we today are the recipients of.

Historic Notes on the Art Rendered in This Book

Page 4: Washington in uniform during the Revolutionary War.
Page 8: Washington attended Henry Williams School and had minimal formal education.
Page 14: Washington interned under surveyor George Fairfax.
Page 18: Washington traveled the Ohio Valley and encountered many tribes during the French and Indian War.
Pages 20–21: This scene of 1755 represents fighting during the French and Indian War, in which British general Edward Braddock was killed in Pennsylvania.
Page 24: A session of the Second Continental Congress, which was held from 1775 to 1781.
Page 26: Washington at Valley Forge during the winter of 1777.
Page 28: A scene from the Battle of Yorktown in 1781.
Page 30: Washington on the portico of Mount Vernon looking out over the Potomac.

Bibliography

Brookhiser, Richard. *Founding Father: Rediscovering George Washington*. New York: Free Press, 1997.
Burns, James MacGregor, and Susan Dunn. *George Washington*. New York: Times Books, 2004.
Clark, Harrison. *All Cloudless Glory, Volume One*. New York: Regnery Publishing, 1998.
d'Aulaire, Ingri, and Edgar Parin d'Aulaire. *George Washington*. San Luis Obispo, CA: Beautiful Feet Books, 1996. First published 1936 by Doubleday, Doran.
Flexner, James Thomas. *George Washington*. Boston: Little, Brown, 1965.
Stevenson, Augusta. *George Washington, Our First Leader*. New York: Aladdin Books, 1988.
Warren, Jack D., Jr. *Northern Neck of Virginia Historical Magazine*. December 1999.
Washington, George. *The Journal of Major George Washington*. Williamsburg, VA: Colonial Williamsburg Foundation, 1754.

THEODORE

FRANK KEATING

PAINTINGS BY
MIKE WIMMER

A PAULA WISEMAN BOOK
Simon & Schuster Books for Young Readers
New York London Toronto Sydney New Delhi

To Catie, Hadley, and Will, the first in a fun line of grandchildren. May they be patriots and hardy lovers of the legacy of Theodore Roosevelt.

—F. K.

Dedicated to my family; like it was for Theodore Roosevelt, it is their love and support that has inspired me and nurtured my God-given abilities to help me achieve all that I am capable of.

"Greatness is destined to be carved in stone."

—M.W.

Acknowledgments

The author and publisher gratefully acknowledge the assistance of the Theodore Roosevelt Association, the Theodore Roosevelt birthplace in New York City, and Wallace Dailey at the Theodore Roosevelt Collection at Harvard College Library in creating this book.

The illustrator gratefully acknowledges Wallace Dailey of the Theodore Roosevelt Collection at Harvard University, Dr. John A. Gable of the Theodore Roosevelt Association, the staff of the Oyster Bay Roosevelt home, and the staff of the Theodore Roosevelt birthplace in New York City.

SIMON & SCHUSTER BOOKS FOR YOUNG READERS
An imprint of Simon & Schuster Children's Publishing Division
1230 Avenue of the Americas, New York, New York 10020

The text for this book is set in Regula.
The paintings for this book are rendered in oil on canvas.
Manufactured in Guangdong province, China
0421 SCP
First Simon & Schuster Books for Young Readers POB proprietary edition April 2021
2 4 6 8 10 9 7 5 3 1
CIP data for this book is available from the Library of Congress.
ISBN: 978-0-689-86532-9

All quotations are the words of Theodore Roosevelt.

Selected Bibliography

Auchincloss, Louis. *Theodore Roosevelt.* New York: Times Books, 2002.
Brands, H. W. *T.R., The Last Romantic.* New York: Basic Books, 1997.

"No ability, no strength and force, no power of intellect or power of wealth, shall avail us, if we have not the root of right living in us."

Theodore Roosevelt

My mother named me Theodore, but everyone remembers me as Teddy.

I grew up to be big and broad and strong. As a man I led a nation to greatness. Some said that I was born to greatness.

It was not quite that way.

I was not born big or strong.

But I did know what I wanted and worked at it every day. My goal was to do big things.

"The best prize that life offers is the chance to work hard at work worth doing," I believed.

I was born on October 27, 1858, in New York City, the second of four children.

As a child I was frail. My health frequently kept me indoors. There I read and dreamed to the farthest faraways of my imagination.

"I was nervous and timid."

But reading about the people I admired from history, the soldiers of Valley Forge and Morgan's Riflemen, filled me with excitement and hope.

My illness made me more determined. I wanted to be strong, like the heroes of America's past about whom I had read.

"I felt a great admiration for men who were fearless and who could hold their own in the world, and I had a great desire to be like them."

ADVENTURES

While my friends played, I created a special world in my mind. I was fascinated by all living things.

When I was seven, I wrote about the size and shape of a seal I had seen in a fish market.

I was full of curiosity and wonder at all creatures great and small.

When I was nine, I composed a "Natural History on Insects," in which I described an assortment of ants, spiders, ladybugs, fireflies, beetles, and dragonflies.

My mother and I were great friends.

"I jumped with delight when I found you had heard a mockingbird," I wrote to her. "Get some of its feathers if you can."

When I was ten, I started to keep a diary. Reading was my routine, and studying and thinking were as normal to me as sleeping and eating.

I loved to read. I read biographies, histories, and books on birds and all things that walk or crawl.

"I remembered a book that I had read sometime ago . . . the pages of the book came before my eyes."

Without fail I kept up my studies and carefully observed nature's wonders around me.

By age eleven I had seen many things. I had traveled to Europe with my family, climbed an eight-thousand-foot mountain, and taken long walks of up to nineteen miles. My father was my best friend and hiking partner. Nothing could keep me from his side.

My mother was proud of the growth of my mind. My father insisted that I strengthen my body. I worked hard at both.

I had boundless energy.

My family traveled to Egypt and the Holy Land, where I catalogued and observed zebras, waders, ziczacs, kites, vultures, and water buffalo.

There was so much to learn. I wanted to know everything and understand all that I saw.

By age fifteen I had sailed to Britain, Europe, North Africa, and the Middle East. I had hunted jackals on horseback, climbed the Great Pyramid, and peered into a volcano.

It was fun. "Isn't this bully?" I exclaimed to my brothers and sisters.

Life with my family was great excitement, a glorious mixture of colors and quests, of drama and dreams.

"I have never spent an unhappy day." I made every day count.

I had many heroes, and I read about the people I most admired—people I wanted to become. They were lovers of freedom.

While still in my twenties I wrote books about the westward expansion; the Naval War of 1812; and American heroes, including biographies of Thomas Hart Benton and Gouverneur Morris. I wrote thirty-five books in all, always celebrating "the joy of life and the duty of life."

"I'm happiest with books all around me."

I worked hard.

Before I was thirty, I headed west—to Dakota Territory and the Little Missouri River, the badlands where the crack of a whip and the steady gait of a horse's hooves were constant sounds in a place lonely and forbidding.

"If you are afraid of hard work . . . do not come west," I wrote to a friend.

My life was the cattle business: wrestling steers; taming ponies; branding calves; and riding, roping, and hunting with the strongest and most experienced of men.

"There are few sensations I prefer to those of galloping over those rolling, limitless prairies."

I hunted and rode, delighting in "the hardy life of the open."

My life was always an adventure.

Hermit thrushes, grosbeaks, robins, bluebirds, thrashers, sparrows, meadowlarks, and whippoorwills all excited my interest. Nature was "the romance of my life."

"I am going cattle ranching. . . . What I shall do after that I cannot tell you."

I was a hunter.

I was the father of six children.

"I play with the children almost every night." Alice. Ted. Kermit. Ethel. Archie. Quentin. Life at the Roosevelt house was a lively jumble of wrestling, running, shouting, and song. I was always in the thick of all the children's mischief. Later, when I ascended to the nation's highest office, a friend humorously remarked, "The president is about six."

I was a soldier.

When the Spanish-American War came, I was ready. My charge up San Juan Hill, into the flash and fury of screeching shells and screaming combat, brought me fame and the nation's highest award for bravery in combat, the Congressional Medal of Honor.

Those events led me to become president of the United States at forty-two, the youngest man ever to hold that office. But the presidency was only the last event of a lifetime of study and service. Legislator. Civil service commissioner. Police commissioner. Assistant secretary of the Navy. Governor of New York. Vice president of the United States.

Great success came from great effort and big dreams.

My life as a father and as a president taught me to face every challenge with energy and integrity.

"It is character that counts in a nation as in a man."

UNUM

I was a builder.

I built my life. I also built a family and a better country.

"It is always better to be an original than an imitation."

I constantly strove to be an original.

I followed my heart wherever it led me.

It was a "worthy course"—to be a better person and to make a better land.

That was the life I lived.

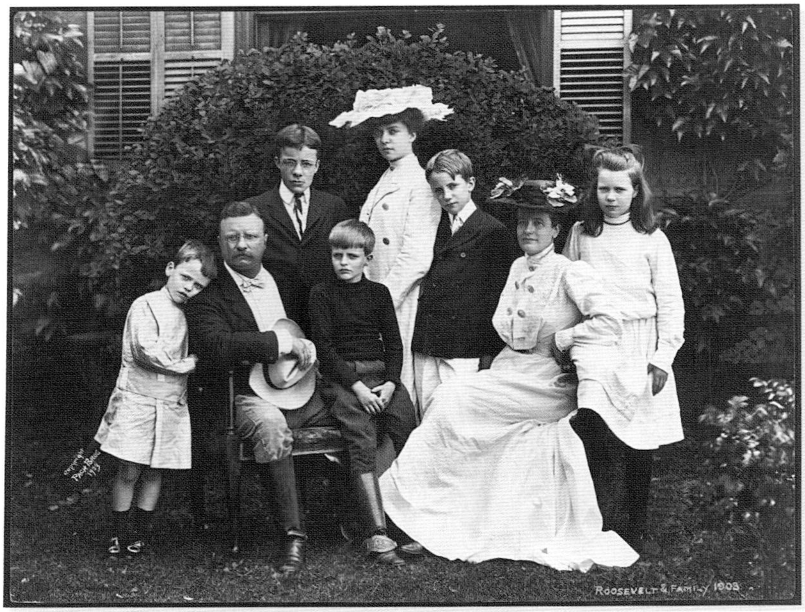

The Roosevelt family (left to right): Quentin, Theodore Roosevelt, Theodore Jr., Archie, Alice, Kermit, Edith Roosevelt, Ethel (Theodore Roosevelt Collection, Harvard College Library)

Theodore Roosevelt (1858–1919) was the twenty-sixth president of the United States. He was born in New York City on October 27, 1858, the second of four children of Theodore and Martha Bulloch Roosevelt. Afflicted with asthma and weak eyes as a young boy, Roosevelt did not let his poor health prevent him from learning and being physically fit. After graduating from Harvard in 1880, he married Alice Hathaway Lee of Chestnut Hill, Massachusetts. She passed away in 1884, leaving one daughter, Alice Lee. Theodore Roosevelt then married Edith Kermit Carow and they had five more children together.

In 1881 Theodore Roosevelt ran for the New York State Legislature and won, holding the office of assemblyman for two terms. In 1884 he purchased a cattle ranch in the badlands of the Dakota Territory, where he lived for two years before returning to New York. There he was defeated in his run for mayor of New York City. Later he organized a group called the Rough Riders, the first U.S. Volunteer Cavalry Regiment, which became nationally known. In 1898 Roosevelt was elected governor of New York. In 1900 Roosevelt accepted the Republican vice-presidential nomination and was elected vice president of the United States. Then, at age forty-two, when fate intervened and President McKinley was assassinated, Roosevelt became president. During his tenure he saw the construction of the Panama Canal and he received the Nobel Peace Prize.

Roosevelt died in his home in Oyster Bay, New York, on January 6, 1919.